MW00807149

TABLE OF CONTENTS

Novel-Ties® are printed on recycled paper.

Copyright © 2002, 2020 by LEARNING LINKS

For the Teacher

This reproducible study guide consists of instructional material to use in conjunction with a specific novel. Written in chapter-by-chapter format, the guide contains a synopsis, pre-reading activities, vocabulary and comprehension exercises, as well as extension activities to be used as follow-up to the novel.

NOVEL-TIES are either for whole class instruction using a single title or for group instruction where each group uses a different novel appropriate to its reading level. Depending upon the amount of time allotted to it in the classroom, each novel, with its guide and accompanying lessons, may be completed in two to four weeks.

The first step in using NOVEL-TIES is to distribute to each student a copy of the novel and a folder containing all of the duplicated worksheets. Begin instruction by selecting several pre-reading activities in order to set the stage for the reading ahead. Vocabulary exercises for each chapter always precede the reading so that new words will be reinforced in the context of the book. Use the questions on the chapter worksheets for class discussion or as written exercises.

The benefits of using NOVEL-TIES are numerous. Students read good literature in the original, rather than in abridged or edited form. The good reading habits formed by practice in focusing on interpretive comprehension and literary techniques will be transferred to the books students read independently. Passive readers become active, avid readers.

SYNOPSIS

Angela's Ashes spans two decades in the life of an Irish Catholic family, during the period from the Great Depression of the 1930s to the 1950s. In this autobiographical work, the narrator and central character is Frank, the eldest child of Malachy and Angela McCourt, born during his parents' brief sojourn in America. Tragedy strikes the family when their baby Margaret dies in their Brooklyn tenement, and Angela's grief becomes a bout of depression. The impoverished young couple are shipped back to Ireland by indignant relatives when alcoholic Malachy McCourt cannot support his wife and their three young sons.

Back in Ireland, the McCourts move from hovel to hovel while Malachy McCourt drinks away his paychecks. The family comes to depend largely on charity and government assistance. Although their twin sons die of pneumonia, Angela continues to conceive and bear children. Little Frank and his brothers attend a Catholic school run by strict masters who try to instill the fear of God in their pupils, but the boys learn less at school than in the streets of the town of Limerick. There they are taught by circumstances to scrabble for coal, steal food, and dodge neighborhood tyrants. At home, their father teaches them to despise the English and the Protestants and to glory in Irish heroes, mythological and historical. These are the lessons that shape Frank McCourt's youth, until he discovers the world of literature.

The family's circumstances decline further when Malachy goes to England in search of work and abdicates his responsibilities to his dependents. Young Frank McCourt becomes the breadwinner when he gets a job delivering telegrams. Finally, there is food to eat and some sense of financial security. Yet, when faced with the opportunity to become a postal employee and earn a living wage, Frank makes a momentous decision: he will emigrate to the United States and carve out his way in the land of opportunity. The book ends with the nineteen-year-old author on American soil, about to discover a land where customs and values are strikingly different from those of his native country.

BACKGROUND INFORMATION

The Creation of the Irish Free State

Modern Irish history has been plagued by conflicts between religious and political factions. These tensions date back to the seventeenth century, when the Protestants gained ascendancy over the Catholics and enforced Penal Laws denying them property and power. In 1800, the English Parliament responded to rebellions in Ireland by coercing the Irish Parliament to pass an Act of Union that ended Irish independence.

Nineteenth-century patriots such as Charles Parnell formed an Irish nationalist party whose major demands were home rule and land reform. This party's program was immensely popular with Catholics. The Protestant elite of Northern Ireland, however, clung to ties with England. Under great pressure, the English Parliament promised home rule for Ireland, but delayed its enactment. Factors such as the famous 1916 Easter Rising, political pressure from radicals of the Sinn Fein party, and prolonged guerrilla warfare by the Irish Republican Army finally resulted in the 1920 Government of Ireland Act. While the law decreed separate parliaments for the North and South of Ireland, only the Northern parliament functioned.

Meanwhile, the violence continued in Ireland. During the 1921 ceasefire, a treaty was enacted that made the South a self-governing territory within the British Commonwealth. The Northern Ireland Parliament broke away from the rest of the country. The treaty was not accepted by all factions, and civil war broke out. Michael Collins led the pro-treaty faction, while Eamon De Valera led the opposition. Collins's pro-treaty faction prevailed.

In this way, the southern twenty counties of Ireland became the Irish Free State with William Thomas Cosgrave as its first prime minister. Problems did not end there. De Valera resisted Cosgrave's government because of the mandatory oath of allegiance to the British government. In 1932, De Valera's Fianna Fail party formed a government, and De Valera became its prime minister. Fianna Fail eventually became more powerful than Cosgrave's Fine Gael party. The 1937 Irish constitution created the state of Eire (formally the Irish Free State) which remained part of the British Commonwealth.

PRE-READING ACTIVITIES

1. Preview the book by reading the title, author's name, and publisher's blurb, and by looking at the illustration on the cover. Noticing that this is a memoir, what do you think the book will be about? What is the setting of the book? Based upon what you know about this setting, do you expect this to be a book of pleasant or difficult memories?

2. Read the Background Information on page two of this study guide and do some additional research to learn about the political and religious tensions in modern Ireland.

   Do some specific research to find out about the following topics:
   • Irish Republican Army
   • British rule over Northern Ireland
   • Catholic minorities in Ireland
   • Wealth and class in modern Ireland
   • Irish emigration in the nineteenth and twentieth centuries

3. With a partner, discuss how a childhood of poverty in a dysfunctional family might be portrayed in a manner that would be upbeat rather than terribly depressing. As you read, monitor those aspects of Frank McCourt's style that serve to lighten the mood of the book.

4. What individuals or institutions have the greatest influence on your life? In the "You" column number the following (with 1 being the most important and 4 being the least important):

You	Author
☐ parent(s) or guardian	☐ parent(s) or guardian
☐ peers	☐ peers
☐ school	☐ ʃl
☐ religious affiliation	☐ religious affiliation

   After you finish the book, fill in the list for the author. Compare the your list with that of the author.

Pre-Reading Activities (cont.)

5. Most of the characters we meet in *Angela's Ashes* live in terrible poverty. Yet, many of them hold deep religious beliefs. In what ways may people rely on religious faith to ease their sufferings? And conversely, how may adherence to some religious practices inadvertently extend human suffering?

6. *Angela's Ashes* was a winner of the prestigious Pulitzer Prize, one of a group of annual prizes established in 1917 by Joseph Pulitzer, a renowned American journalist and publisher. As you read, try to determine those qualities which contributed to the selection of this book for the Pulitzer Prize.

7. With your classmates discuss books and films that you have encountered that portray Irish Americans or are set in Ireland. What common problems and themes run through all of these works? Why do you think there is such a rich tradition of Irish literature?

CHAPTERS I, II

Vocabulary: Draw a line from each word on the left to its definition on the right. Then use the numbered words to fill in the blanks in the sentences below.

1. cacophony		a. disrespectful act
2. congested		b. lung disease
3. atrocious		c. exceptionally bad
4. consumption		d. clogged
5. sacrilege		e. jarring noise
6. perfidy		f. shortage
7. loquacious		g. rejected
8. scarcity		h. talkative
9. spurned		i. disloyalty

. . . .

1. The patient's _____ nasal passages made breathing extremely uncomfortable.

2. The medical condition once known as _____ killed many people prior to the discovery of antibiotics.

3. The proud nobility of Europe _____ the peasants whose backbreaking labor provided food for the kingdom.

4. The music teacher covered her ears at the _____ of untuned violins, violas, and cellos.

5. To some deeply religious persons, arguing with a priest is a(n) _____.

6. The doctor's handwriting was so _____, his patients could hardly read their prescriptions.

7. To betray a person or a country is an act of _____.

8. Once the movie begins, we hope your _____ friends will stop talking.

9. In times of famine, there is a(n) _____ of food.

Chapters I, II (cont.)

Questions:

1. Why did the author believe that the misery of his own childhood was worse than other miserable childhoods?

2. Why did the author's father emigrate from Ireland to the United States?

3. Why do Angela's cousins refer to Malachy McCourt as a Presbyterian?

4. Why does Mam sometimes sing romantic songs?

5. How do Frank and his brother Malachy respond to their mother's depression?

6. Why is it difficult for Dad to hold a job?

7. Why is Margaret's death such a tragedy for Frank's family?

8. Why don't Frank and his family stay in Northern Ireland?

9. How does Grandma Sheehan respond when the family arrives in Limerick?

10. Why do the twins die within six months of one another?

11. What does the family's return to Ireland represent for Angela and Malachy McCourt?

Questions for Discussion:

1. Do you think the author remembers his father as a villain or as a victim of circumstance? What evidence supports your opinion?

2. Do you think the aunts were justified in interfering in the lives of Angela, Malachy, and their children?

3. Do you think the poverty Frank's family suffered was a product of the time in which they lived, personal inadequacy, or fate? What resources might be available to them today that were not available then?

4. Why do you think the author contrasts Mrs. Liebowitz and her family with his own family? How do the foods each family feeds its children reflect its status?

5. How does the reception of Frank's family in Ireland make a mockery of his father's patriotism?

Chapters I, II (cont.)

Literary Element: Setting

The setting of a book refers to the time and place in which the events occur. The situations of poor people in urban New York City and rural Limerick, Ireland in the 1930s are compared in the opening chapters of this book. Use a Venn diagram, such as the one below, to compare the living conditions and attitudes of the people in Frank McCourt's life. Record similarities in the overlapping part of the circles.

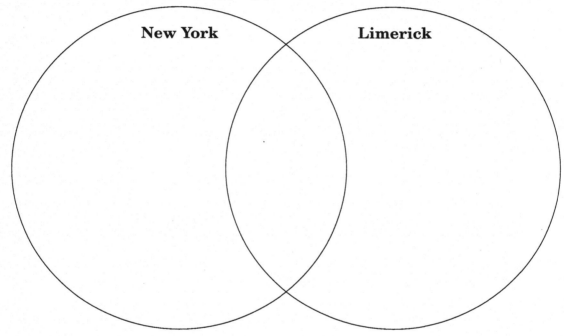

New York   Limerick

Literary Device: Point of View

Point of view refers to the voice telling the story. In this memoir, the author recounts his own childhood. Why do you think he relates most of the story in present tense rather than past tense?

_____

_____

Writing Activities:

1. Imagine a scenario in which Mrs. Liebowitz of Brooklyn meets Grandma Sheehan of Limerick. They have come together to discuss the problems of Angela's family. Write a brief dialogue that expresses the personalities and viewpoints of these two women.

2. Write about a time when a change in family circumstances greatly affected your own way of life. Describe the change and tell whether it had a positive or negative effect.

CHAPTERS III–V

Vocabulary: Use the context to determine the meaning of the underlined word in each of the following sentences. Then use a dictionary to find the exact meaning of the word.

1. The lighthouse keeper kept a lonely <u>vigil</u> during the stormy night.

    Your definition _____

    Dictionary definition _____

2. The nurse administered medication to the <u>afflicted</u> patients on her ward.

    Your definition _____

    Dictionary definition _____

3. The disgraced soldier was imprisoned for <u>collaborating</u> with the enemy troops.

    Your definition _____

    Dictionary definition _____

4. The ancient Greeks believed that their gods and goddesses were <u>immortal</u>.

    Your definition _____

    Dictionary definition _____

5. People will flock to the <u>cinema</u> to see a film starring their favorite actors.

    Your definition _____

    Dictionary definition _____

6. The bull, stung by a horde of wasps, bucked and twisted in a <u>demented</u> manner.

    Your definition _____

    Dictionary definition _____

7. The accused man's reputation was <u>redeemed</u> by the supportive testimony of a new witness.

    Your definition _____

    Dictionary definition _____

8. During the famine, men, women, and children were <u>expiring</u> by the thousands.

    Your definition _____

    Dictionary definition _____

Chapters III–V (cont.)

Questions:

1. Why does the family move from their room on Hartstonge Street?

2. Why is it difficult for Dad to get a job in Limerick?

3. Why do Mam and Dad refer to the downstairs of their dwelling on Roden Lane as "Ireland" and the upstairs as "Italy"?

4. How does Grandma Sheehan regard the pig's head Mam secures for the family's Christmas dinner?

5. Why are the children of Limerick eager to make their First Confession and First Communion?

6. Why does Frank admire Mikey Molloy?

7. Why is Frank surprised by the priest's reaction to his First Confession?

8. Why is Grandma Sheehan outraged when young Frank vomits up his breakfast on the day of his First Communion?

9. How is Frank able to attend the cinema for three consecutive Saturdays?

Questions for Discussion:

1. Do you think there is any justification for Dad's pride in appearance and refusal to seek help from charitable organizations?

2. Why do you think the boys at Frank's school are so harsh in their teasing of one another?

3. Why do you think the adults in Frank's world do not welcome the questions of children?

4. How do the attitudes of professionals, such as doctors and social workers, compound the problems of poverty that Frank and his family face?

5. From what you have read so far, how would you assess Frank's feelings about the religion of his childhood?

6. What does the attitude of the people in Limerick toward the "soupers" reveal about Catholic/Protestant relations?

7. What does Frank's rejection by the sacristan at St. Joseph's reveal about the class structure of Limerick, Ireland during the 1930s and '40s?

Chapters III–V (cont.)

Literary Devices:

I. *Symbolism* — A symbol in literature is an object, a person, or an event that represents an idea or a set of ideas. What may each of the following symbolize:

- pig's head
- picture of the Pope
- bird that drinks Cuchulain's blood

II. *Sarcasm* — Sarcasm refers to remarks that are bitter or derisive. It is often a cruel form of humor that ridicules its victim. For example:

> They [the women] don't sit because all they do is stay at home, take care of the children, clean the house and cook a bit and the men need more chairs. The men sit because they're worn out from walking to the Labour Exchange every morning to sign for the dole,...

What does the author really mean?

_____

_____

Find another example of sarcasm.

_____

_____

III. *Irony* — Irony of situation refers to events that turn out to be the opposite of what is expected. Describe the ironies that occur on Frank's First Communion day.

_____

_____

_____

_____

Chapters III–V (cont.)

IV. *Comic Relief* — Comic relief refers to an episode of humor set within otherwise serious prose. How do the episodes about Mam and Dad's teeth provide some degree of comic relief?

_____

_____

_____

What other episodes provide comic relief?

_____

_____

_____

Writing Activity:

Recall an incident when you were young in which you or someone you know was humiliated by adults or taunted by your peers. Describe the incident and tell how it affected future attitudes and behavior.

CHAPTERS VI–VIII

Vocabulary: Use the context to help you choose the best meaning for the underlined word in each of the following sentences. Then circle the letter of the definition you choose.

1. The <u>froth</u> on the surface of the pond revealed that there were living things under the water.

   a. water-lilies   b. foam   c. ripples   d. litter

2. The captain of the oil tanker would <u>rue</u> the day his ship hit the iceberg.

   a. regret   b. recall   c. blame   d. explain

3. Each soldier was issued his rifle and a <u>bandolier</u> to hold his ammunition.

   a. manual   b. uniform   c. cartridge belt   d. paycheck

4. As a <u>penance</u>, the convicted man offered to do community service for a year.

   a. favor   b. self-punishment   c. judgment   d. apology

5. The lost hiker had the <u>fortitude</u> to remain calm until the rescue team found her.

   a. strength   b. patience   c. wit   d. fortune

6. <u>Subtle</u> differences between the two paintings allowed the expert to identify the forgery.

   a. obvious   b. slight   c. major   d. possible

7. The <u>scrawny</u> horse could barely pull the heavy wagon up the hill.

   a. sweaty   b. elderly   c. bony   d. stubborn

8. The weight of evidence <u>induced</u> the jury to acquit the accused woman.

   a. persuaded   b. argued   c. frightened   d. pleaded

Chapters VI–VIII (cont.)

Questions:

1. Why doesn't Frank return to school after spending lunchtime at Fintan's house?

2. What evidence reveals the degree of poverty that Paddy Clohessy's family experiences?

3. How does Frank begin to realize the seriousness of his father's alcoholism?

4. How do the children respond to Dad when he spends the dole money on alcohol?

5. Why does Frank fight with Declan Collopy?

6. Why can't Frank ask his parents questions about childbirth?

7. Why is Mam desperate to baptize the new baby, Alphie?

8. Why does Frank remain untreated during the early stages of typhoid fever?

9. Why does Sister Rita of the Fever Hospital separate Frank and Patricia Madigan?

10. Why doesn't Seamus think *The Amazing Quest of Mr. Ernest Bliss* is a realistic novel?

Questions for Discussion:

1. How would you assess Mr. O'Neill's skill as a teacher? What does his disposal of the apple peels reveal about his degree of sensitivity?

2. How might the Clohessy family have saved Frank from getting into trouble with his mother?

3. Why do you think Frank becomes so attached to Mr. Timoney? How does he differ from all the other adults in Frank's life?

4. Why do you think the priest offers Frank forgiveness when he confesses to theft?

5. Which of Dad's qualities do you think make him lovable in Frank's eyes, despite his inadequacy as a provider?

6. In what ways does the hospital experience and the recuperative period afterwards open up new possibilities in life for Frank?

7. As revealed in this book, do you think that religion in Ireland offered comfort and support or held people back from overcoming their difficulties?

Chapters VI–VIII (cont.)

Literary Device: Allusion

Allusion — An allusion in literature is a reference to persons, places, events, or literary titles or quotations whose identities the reader is expected to recognize.

Read the entire text of Jonathan Swift's *A Modest Proposal* to discover why Mr. Timoney might have wanted Frank to read it to him.

Literary Element: Vernacular

A writer uses vernacular, the nonstandard language of a particular region, to capture the way people actually speak. For example:

"Ah, no, me nose is bleedin'."

Throughout the novel, the author's decision to reproduce the characters' speech in the vernacular underscores the authenticity, or realism, of the story. What are some other examples of vernacular that you can find in this section of the novel?

_____

_____

_____

_____

Science Connection:

Do some research to learn about the illness once referred to as consumption, but now called tuberculosis. Learn how this contagious disease once decimated entire populations and how it was once treated. Then find out how the disease is treated today and whether it presents a medical threat today.

Author's Style:

Why do you think Frank McCourt relates the events of his life story in straightforward language without expressing his opinions of the people and world around him? How does he expect the reader to draw conclusions about his family and the place and times in which he lived?

Writing Activity:

Imagine that you are a visitor to Limerick, Ireland, in the 1930s. Write a letter to the editor of an Irish newspaper in which you describe and protest health conditions among the poor.

CHAPTERS IX–XII

Vocabulary: Use the words in the Word Box and the clues below to complete the cross-word puzzle.

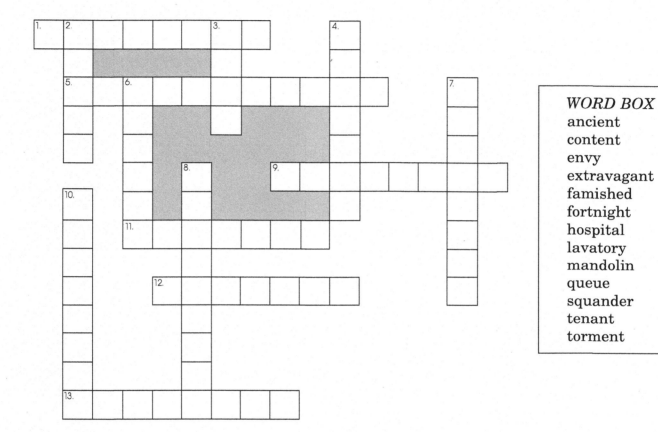

WORD BOX
ancient
content
envy
extravagant
famished
fortnight
hospital
lavatory
mandolin
queue
squander
tenant
torment

Across

1. spend or use money wastefully
5. spending much more than is necessary or wise
9. musical instrument with a pear-shaped wooden body and neck like a guitar
11. afflict great bodily or emotional pain
12. of or in time long past
13. bathroom

Down

2. line of people waiting their turn
3. have feelings of resentment toward someone who has what one wishes to possess
4. satisfied with what one is or has
6. person or group who rents land or living space from another
7. extremely hungry
8. two weeks
10. institution for the care and treatment of the sick and wounded

Chapters IX–XII (cont.)

Questions:

1. Why did many Limerick men leave Ireland for England during the 1940s?

2. Why does Mam have mixed reactions to Dad's departure for Coventry, England?

3. What is the effect of Dad's prolonged absence on the rest of the family?

4. What happens at the Dispensary to further lower Mam's self-respect? How does she attempt to restore her dignity?

5. Why do Frank and his brothers have to move in with Aunt Aggie, their mother's sister who despises them?

6. What causes Frank to rise in the estimation of the local boys of Limerick?

7. How does Dad's Christmas visit contradict his claim that he is a changed man?

8. How does Frank come to appreciate Shakespeare and yearn to live in America?

9. Why does Laman Griffin allow Mam and the children to move into his house?

Questions for Discussion:

1. What do the wishes that Mam expresses upon her husband's departure for England reveal about her life?

2. The author describes his interactions with men such as Pa Keating, Mr. Hannon, and the signal master at the Limerick train station. What do you think young Frank learned from these men? How do their values and behavior compare with those of the author's father?

3. Do you think there is any justification for the way Mr. Coffey and Mr. Kane treat the people who come for public assistance? What emotional and physical toll do you think their treatment has upon its victims?

4. How do you think Frank's feelings about his mother change after he sees her begging in the streets? Do you think his feelings are justified? Might he have reacted in another way?

5. The boys who attend school with Frank are eager to find full-time jobs by the time they are fourteen or fifteen. What do you think the long-term effect of this lack of higher education will be for these boys? How does this situation determine their futures?

Chapters IX–XII (cont.)

6. Why do you think the people that Frank knows in Limerick are disinterested in the World War that is raging?

7. How does Frank's impoverished appearance, as he compares himself to the boys who attend the Jesuit School, reinforce his understanding of the strict class divisions that exist in Ireland?

Science Connection:

Do some research to learn about conjunctivitis, the disease that affected Frank's eyes. Learn about its causes, symptoms, and current treatment. Also, determine why it is no longer as serious a disease as it was during Frank's youth.

Literary Devices:

I. *Hyperbole* — Hyperbole refers to exaggeration used for effect. Hyperbole dramatizes a situation, often with humorous intent. For example, Aunt Aggie mocks a middle-aged neighbor who still hopes to conceive a child:

> Forty-five she is now and if there's another child we'll have to look for a star in the East.

In this instance of hyperbole, the neighbor is mockingly compared to Mary, the mother of Jesus. In the New Testament, a star in the East announced Jesus' birth. Thus, the birth of a child to this neighbor would be a miracle.

Record another example of hyperbole. Indicate the page on which it appeared.

_____

_____

II. *Irony* — What is ironic about the doctor's suggestion that Frank build up his health by eating "plenty of beef and eggs" when he returns home from the hospital.

_____

_____

III. *Symbolism* — What did the football goal symbolize for Frank?

_____

_____

Chapters IX–XII (cont.)

Literary Element: Characterization

The character of Angela is slowly being drawn by her own actions and reactions and by the comments of other characters as they observe her or remember her past. Choose five descriptive words that best reflect her character. Record them in the character web below and provide one example to substantiate your choice of adjective. Compare your responses with those of your classmates.

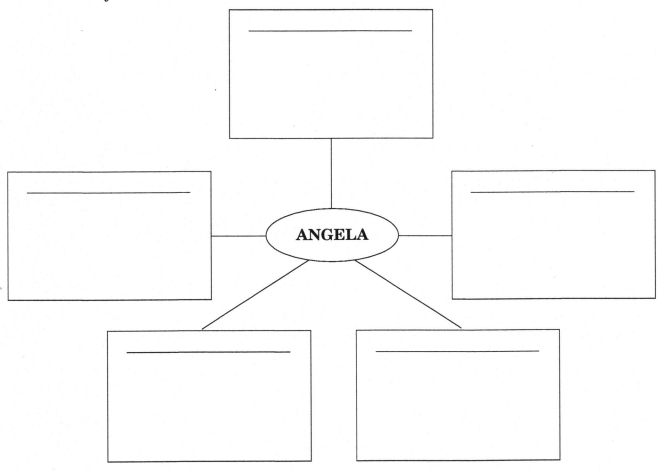

From what you have learned about Angela, how has she changed since her marriage?

Writing Activities:

1. Write about a time when an adult in your life disappointed you or did not live up to your expectations. Tell whether you ever came to terms with your feelings of disappointment.

2. Write about a time when someone helped you over a difficult hurdle, or gave you courage to face a challenge. What was especially memorable about this incident and the person who helped you?

CHAPTERS XIII–XV

Vocabulary: Analogies are equations in which the first pair of words has the same relationship as the second pair of words. For example: ENORMOUS is to HUGE as ENTERTAIN is to AMUSE. Both pairs of words are synonyms. Choose the best word from the Word Box to complete each of the analogies below.

	WORD BOX	
adroit	pithy	rustics
dismal	resplendent	succumb
inviolate	revile	vanquished

1. MOIST is to DRY as WORDY is to _____.

2. PRAISE is to COMPLIMENT as _____ is to DENOUNCE.

3. URBANITES is to CITY as _____ is to COUNTRYSIDE.

4. LABOR is to RELAX as _____ is to RESIST.

5. _____ is to BRILLIANT as CRUDE is to RAW.

6. CALM is to PEACEFUL as _____ is to DEFT.

7. _____ is to PROFANED as WHOLE is to BROKEN.

8. DECENT is to PROPER as _____ is to GLOOMY.

9. VICTORIOUS is to JUBILATION as _____ is to DESPONDENCY.

Questions:

1. Why does Laman Griffin renege on his promise to lend Frank the bicycle for the cycling trip to Killaloe? What does this reveal about Griffin's character?

2. Why does Mr. O'Halloran, the seventh-class teacher, insist that the students memorize the poem, "The Deserted Village"?

3. Why does Brother Murray of the Christian Brothers immediately reject Frank as a candidate for placement in the school?

4. Why does Frank leave Laman's house, where his mother and brothers still live?

5. What must Frank do in order to survive his stay at his Uncle Ab Sheehan's house? By what means does he avoid starving?

6. Why are telegrams eagerly awaited in the poor lanes of Limerick?

7. How does Frank's job change the lives of his mother and brothers?

Chapters XIII–XV (cont.)

Questions for Discussion:

1. Do you think Angela should have allowed herself to be victimized by her husband and later by Laman? Were there any other paths she might have taken?

2. Why do you think Aunt Aggie buys Frank clothes for his new job as a telegram messenger?

3. Which factors do you think most powerfully influence Frank's plans for the future? Which people are particularly influential in his decision to emigrate to America?

4. How do you think Frank's job as messenger enhances his knowledge of the world?

5. Do you think Frank should have violated Post Office regulations by doing personal errands for the people to whom he delivers telegrams? What does his behavior toward these people suggest about his character?

6. How do the religious teachings to which Frank has been exposed affect his reaction to Theresa Carmody's death?

Literary Devices:

I. *Simile* — A simile is a figure of speech in which two objects are compared using the words "like" or "as." For example:

> Other backyards have lines with clothes that are bright and colorful
> and dance in the wind. Mine hang from the line like dead dogs.

Why is this an apt comparison?

_____

_____

II. *Point of View* — Why do you think the author describes most of the characters and events in the book from a child's point of view? How has the perspective changed during the course of the book? How would this memoir be different if McCourt editorialized or commented on people and situations from an adult's point of view?

_____

_____

_____

_____

Writing Activity:

Write about an event from your early childhood that impressed itself on your memory. Describe this event as a child would do, without editorialization or commentary.

CHAPTERS XVI–XIX

Vocabulary: Antonyms are words with opposite meanings. Draw a line from each word in column A to its antonym in column B. Then use the words in column A to complete the sentences below.

<u>A</u>

1. assiduity
2. languish
3. repose
4. intercede
5. absolution
6. cherish
7. perseverance

<u>B</u>

a. condemnation
b. restlessness
c. despise
d. flightiness
e. indolence
f. prosper
g. avoid

. . . .

1. Our mother taught us to _____ and respect family members and to openly express that love.

2. Owing to the _____ of the clerk, our documents were authorized correctly and swiftly.

3. It takes a wise person to know when to _____ in a disagreement and when to withdraw from the fray.

4. In the classic fairytale, it is the valor and _____ of the hero that allows him to conquer the most overwhelming obstacles.

5. The exhausted children fell asleep immediately, and only the morning sun disturbed their _____.

6. The miserly uncle would not aid his poor relatives, but let them _____ in their poverty and despair.

7. In some religions, a holy person is empowered to grant _____ to those who have admitted their errors.

Chapters XVI–XIX (cont.)

Questions:

1. Why does Frank get his job back at the Post Office? What does this reveal about the power of the Catholic Church in Limerick?

2. How does Mrs. Finucane manage to keep up the pretense that she writes her own threatening letters to delinquent customers?

3. Why does Uncle Pa Keating discourage Frank from taking the permanent exam that would qualify him for a job as a postman?

4. As Frank applies for a job at Easons, why does Mr. McCaffrey make an issue out of Frank living in a lane?

5. How does the Franciscan priest help lift a burden of guilt from Frank?

6. As a magazine and newspaper distributor, how does Mr. McCaffrey practice censorship? Why does he do so?

7. Why does Frank throw Mrs. Finucane's ledger into the river? What need of Frank's does this action serve?

Questions for Discussion:

1. What is the underlying cause of Mr. Harrington's rage? Why do you think he directs it at Frank?

2. What talents does Frank discover in himself during his adolescence? How do these gifts prepare him to become a writer?

3. Compare the behaviors for which Frank feels sinful and those whose possible sin he ignores. What does this reveal about his values and education?

4. Do you believe that Frank was justified in taking the money from Mrs. Finucane's hoard after her death?

5. Why do you think the narrative concludes with Frank aboard the ship?

6. The final chapter of the novel contains a single word, " 'Tis." Why do you think the author chose to end the book in this way?

Chapters XVI–XIX (cont.)

Literary Element: Characterization

I. In *Angela's Ashes*, the author employs an understated style, one in which actions—and characters—speak for themselves. It is up to the reader to form an opinion of the characters, based on their behavior and manner of self-expression. Use the chart below to list at least three descriptive words about some of the main characters in the novel. Compare your responses with those of your classmates.

Characters	Adjectives
Frank	
Dad	
Mam	
Uncle Pa	
Aunt Aggie	
Grandma Sheehan	
Malachy (Frank's brother)	

II. What traits of character did Frank possess that allowed him to break away from the squalor of Ireland and move toward his dream of living in America?

_____

_____

_____

Chapters XVI–XIX (cont.)

Literary Devices:

I. *Irony* — What is ironic about Frank sending letters to Mrs. Finucane's delinquent customers?

_____

_____

What is ironic about the fire in Mr. McCaffrey's magazine distribution office?

_____

_____

_____

II. *Symbolism* — What do the doors that are literally slammed in Frank's face symbolize?

_____

_____

_____

_____

Writing Activity:

Imagine you are Frank and write a letter home, or a diary entry reflecting your perceptions of the world you meet when you arrive in America.

CLOZE ACTIVITY

The following passage has been taken from Chapter Twelve. Read it through completely and then fill in each blank with a word that makes sense. Afterwards, you may compare your language with that of the author.

     There's a letter from Dad. He's coming home two days before Christmas.

_____[1] says everything will be different, he's a _____[2] man,

he hopes we're good boys, obeying _____[3] mother, attending to our religious

duties, and _____[4] bringing us all something for Christmas.

     Mam _____[5] me to the railway station to meet _____.[6]

The station is always exciting with all _____[7] coming and going, people

leaning from carriages, _____[8] smiling, waving good-bye, the train hooting

and _____,[9] chugging away in clouds of steam, people _____[10]

on the platform, the railway tracks silvering _____[11] the distance, on to

Dublin and the _____[12] beyond.

     Now it's near midnight and cold _____[13] the empty platform. A

man in a _____[14] cap asks us if we'd like to _____[15] in a

warm place. Mam says, Thank _____[16] very much, and laughs when he

leads _____[17] to the end of the platform where _____[18] have

to climb a ladder to the _____[19] tower. It takes her a while because

_____[20] heavy and she keeps saying, Oh, God, _____,[21] God.

     We're above the world and it's _____[22] in the signal tower except

for the _____[23] that blink red and green and yellow _____[24]

the man bends over the board. He _____,[25] I'm just having a bit of supper

_____[26] you're welcome.

     Mam says, Ah, no, thanks, _____[27] couldn't take your supper

from you.

He _____,²⁸ The wife always makes too much for

_____²⁹ and if I was up in this _____³⁰ for a week I wouldn't

be able _____³¹ eat it. Sure it's not hard work _____³² at

lights and pulling on the odd lever.

He takes the top off a flask _____³³ pours cocoa into a mug. Here,

he _____³⁴ to me, put yourself outside that cocoa.

_____³⁵ hands Mam half a sandwich. Ah, no, _____³⁶

says, surely you could take that home _____³⁷ your children.

I have two sons, missus, _____³⁸ they're off there fighting in the

forces _____³⁹ His Majesty, the King of England. One

_____⁴⁰ his bit with Montgomery in Africa and _____⁴¹ other is

over in Burma or some _____⁴² bloody place, excuse the language. We get

_____⁴³ freedom from England and then we fight _____⁴⁴

wars. So here, missus, take the bit _____⁴⁵ sandwich.

Lights on the board are clicking _____⁴⁶ the man says, Your train

is coming, _____.⁴⁷

Thank you very much and Happy Christmas.

_____⁴⁸ Christmas to yourself, missus, and a Happy

_____⁴⁹ Year, too. Mind yourself on that ladder, _____⁵⁰ fella.

Help your mother.

Thank you very much _____,⁵¹ sir.

We wait again on the platform _____⁵² the train rumbles into the

station. Carriage _____⁵³ open and a few men with suitcases

_____⁵⁴ to the platform and hurry toward the gate. There is a clanking of

milk cans dropped to the platform. A man and two boys are unloading newspapers and

magazines. There is no sign of my father.

POST-READING ACTIVITIES

1. Return to Exercise #4 in the Pre-Reading Activities on page three of this study guide. Fill in the "Author" column and compare it to your own opinion. What are the formative influences shaping the development of the main character? What does he learn through his experiences?

2. Now that you have finished reading the book, why do you think the author chose *Angela's Ashes* for its title?

3. Do some research to learn about Irish history in the decades that follow the time of this novel. Read about politics, religion, and economics in the North and South of Ireland. If possible, find newspaper articles that report on events in Ireland. What issues that Frank McCourt wrote about are still cause for controversy today?

4. In what ways are Frank McCourt's experiences representative of the situation of Ireland's poor? In what respects does his experience seem to differ from that of other impoverished children of rural Ireland during the first half of the twentieth century?

5. Do you think Frank's memories of his father reflect bitterness or love and acceptance? Do you think he ever really forgave his mother for her behavior while living under Laman Griffin's roof?

6. View the movie version of *Angela's Ashes* and compare it with the book. Does the movie capture the texture and emotional depths of the memoir? If there are significant differences between film and written text, discuss how they change your experience.

7. In chapter XIII of the novel, the schoolmaster Mr. O'Halloran tells his class it's a shame that intelligent boys are forced into manual labor. "He is disgusted by this free and independent Ireland that keeps a class system foisted on us by the English, that we are throwing our talented children on the dungheap." On the other hand, Frank's father is constantly citing the glories of his native land and the courage of the Irish heroes. Which of these points of view does Frank come to embrace? What factors contribute to the development of this attitude toward his country and its inhabitants?

8. *Angela's Ashes* derives much of its power from the keenly observed details of its locale. Yet, some of the memoir's themes are universal: the quest of the hero to survive his troubles and triumph over adversity; the endurance of love against the odds and the failure of love; the dilemma of the hero as he struggles to balance individuality with social mores. Discuss one of these themes as it is developed throughout the book.

SUGGESTIONS FOR FURTHER READING

Fiction

Beckett, Samuel. *Molloy/Malone Dies/The Unnamable*. Grove/Atlantic, Inc.

Behan, Brendan. *Borstal Boy*. Nonparieil Books.

Bowen, Elizabeth. *The Last September!* Kindle.

Carlson, Sarah. *All the Walls of Belfast*. Turner.

* Cisneros, Sandra. *House on Mango Street*. Vintage.

Doyle, Roddy. *Paddy Clarke Ha Ha Ha*. Penguin.

Joyce, James. *Dubliners*. Macmillan.

_____. *Portrait of the Artist as a Young Man*. Penguin.

Kent, Hannah. *The Good People*. Back Bay Books.

* Morrison, Toni. *Beloved*. Vintage.

O'Brien, Edna. *The Country Girls*. Farrar, Straus and Giroux.

O'Neill, Eugene. *Long Day's Journey Into Night*. Yale University Press.

Faoláin, Seán Ó. Collected Stories. Little, Brown.

Nonfiction

* Angelou, Maya. *I Know Why The Caged Bird Sings*. Random House.

Ardagh, John. *Ireland and the Irish: Portrait of a Changing Society*. Penguin.

Brown, Terence. *Ireland: A Social and Cultural History 1922–1985*. Harper Perennial.

Coogan, Tim Pat. *The Famine Plot!* St. Martins Griffin.

O'Connor, Frank. *Guests of the Nation*. Irish Books and Media.

* Wright, Richard. *Black Boy*. HarperCollins.

Also by Frank McCourt

Teacher Man! Scribner.

'Tis. Scribner.

* NOVEL-TIES Study Guides are available for these titles.

ANSWER KEY

Chapters I, II

Vocabulary: 1. e 2. d 3. c 4. b 5. a 6. i 7. h 8. f 9. g; 1. congested 2. consumption 3. spurned 4. cacophony 5. sacrilege 6. atrocious 7. perfidy 8. loquacious 9. scarcity

Questions: 1. Frank McCourt believed that the poverty in which his family lived in Ireland, compounded by his father's alcoholism, his mother's depression, and the constraints of the Catholic Church made his childhood particularly miserable. 2. The author's father emigrated from Ireland to the United States because he had been associated with the Irish Republican Army, an illegal organization. If he had been caught by the authorities, he would have been imprisoned. 3. Angela's cousins refer to Malachy McCourt derisively as a Presbyterian because they are Irish Catholics who are extremely intolerant of Protestants. Since they dislike the author's father, they assume he cannot be a Catholic like themselves. 4. Mam sometimes sings romantic songs when Dad is employed and brings home his paycheck; when he proves himself a devoted husband and father, her love for him is rekindled. 5. Frank and his brother Malachy respond to their mother's depression by taking on adult responsibilities, such as changing the twins' diapers, foraging for food, and seeking help from kindly neighbors. They often behave in ways that are mature for their ages, although they are still little boys who get into fights and earn parental disapproval. 6. Dad cannot hold a job for long because he is an alcoholic. When he receives a paycheck, he is liable to spend it in bars, oversleep the next day, and fail to report to work, often causing him to be fired. 7. Margaret's death is a terrible tragedy because Angela had desperately wanted a girl and Frank's father had become so smitten with her that he had ceased drinking while she was alive. 8. Frank and his family do not stay in Northern Ireland because they receive no help with money or a job from either his father's family or the IRA in Dublin. 9. Grandma Sheehan responds to the arrival of Angela's family in Limerick with a sour and disapproving attitude; she helps them with basic necessities, but is openly critical of them. 10. The twins die within six months of each other because they contract pneumonia from the dampness and squalor of their living conditions. 11. The family's return to Ireland represents a closing of financial and social options for Angela and Malachy McCourt, as well as for their children. In the rigid society of Limerick, the McCourts cannot easily improve their circumstances, and are subject to class snobbery.

Chapters III–V

Vocabulary: 1. vigil—watch kept during normal sleeping hours 2. afflicted—suffering 3. collaborating—cooperating reasonably 4. immortal—not subject to death; eternal 5. cinema—movie theater 6. demented—insane 7. redeemed—rescued 8. expiring—dying

Questions: 1. The family moves because Angela cannot bear to live in the place where her twins died. 2. It is difficult for Dad to get a job in Limerick because people identify him as a Northerner by his accent. The townspeople are citizens of the Irish Free State and are violently prejudiced against those from Northern Ireland, who are under the dominion of the English. 3. Mam and Dad refer to the downstairs of their dwelling on Roden Lane as "Ireland" and the upstairs as "Italy" because downstairs is damp and unhealthy, while upstairs is dry and warm like Italy as they imagine it. 4. Grandma Sheehan regards the pig's head Mam secures for the family's Christmas dinner as a shameful object that underscores their extreme poverty and Dad's failure as a provider. 5. The children of Limerick are eager to make their First Confession and First Communion not because of religious conviction but because they can then get a new outfit, collect money from the neighbors, and gain free admission to the local cinema. 6. Frank admires Mikey Molloy because he is more sophisticated than the other neighborhood boys; he passes on information about girls and sexual relationships to the others. 7. Fearing the priest's wrath in response to his story about Cuchulain's marriage, Frank is astonished by his gentle reproach and apparent amusement. 8. Grandma Sheehan is outraged when young Frank vomits up his breakfast on the day of his First Communion because she takes literally the significance of the Communion wafer and cannot see it as a symbol of the host. 9. With the money his mother gives him for Irish dancing class, Frank goes to the cinema instead.

Chapters VI–VIII

Vocabulary: 1. b 2. a 3. c 4. b 5. a 6. b 7. c 8. a

Questions: 1. Frank doesn't return to school because Fintan eats his lunch without sharing it with the two boys he has invited to join him. Instead of returning to school, the two hungry boys pick apples and milk a cow in the fields. 2. After describing the McCourts' abject poverty, the author reveals that the Clohessys' living conditions are even worse: they live in one room in a dilapidated, unsanitary building; they exist close to starvation level; and Mr. Clohessy is dying from untreated consumption. 3. Frank begins to realize the seriousness of his father's alcoholism when he takes money from Grandpa McCourt intended as a gift for the new baby and spends it at the pubs. 4. When Dad spends the dole money on alcohol, the children respond by avoiding him in order to punish him and by siding openly with Mam. 5. Frank fights with Declan Collopy because the latter is a local bully, who uses his association with the Confraternity to muscle other boys into attending meetings. Collopy harasses Frank when he sees that instead of attending a meeting, Frank is delivering papers for his Uncle Pat. 6. Frank cannot ask his parents about childbirth or any sexual matters because they would avoid his questions. In that time and place parents, particularly those who were Catholic, would not discuss these matters with children. 7. Mam is desperate to baptize the new baby because the Catholic Church teaches that unbaptized babies go to Limbo rather than Heaven. Mam is afraid the baby will die and lose his chance of having a happy afterlife. 8. Frank remains untreated during the early stages of typhoid fever because of the ignorance of those around him. Grandma declares he has "growing pains" and the first doctor called in on the case incorrectly diagnoses the disease as a common cold. 9. Sister Rita of the Fever Hospital separates Frank and Patricia because she believes that they will weaken themselves by talking so much. She does not seem to realize that these conversations are helpful to the young patients. 10. Seamus doesn't think that *The Amazing Quest of Mr. Ernest Bliss* is a realistic novel because its main character is a rich man who loses his appetite; in a place where poverty is common, no sane person would refuse to eat a meal.

Chapters IX–XII

Vocabulary: Across—1. squander 5. extravagant 9. mandolin 11. torment 12. ancient 13. lavatory; Down—2. queue 3. envy 4. content 6. tenant 7. famished 8. fortnight 10. hospital

Questions: 1. Many Limerick men left Ireland, where there was a paucity of jobs, to go to England where there were jobs in the munitions factories. During World War II, the increase in industry caused factories to hire many extra workers. 2. Mam reacts to Dad's departure with ambivalent feelings; she is both desperate for him to earn money to support the family, and grieved that the family will not be together. 3. The effect of Dad's prolonged absence is to plunge the family into poverty and degradation, as he sends no money home and cannot be forced to turn over any of his wages to Mam. 4. At the Dispensary, Mam's self-respect is reduced by the sarcastic, contemptuous attitude of Mr. Kane; he first implies that Mam must have money from abroad, then speculates that Dad spends all his money on vices, and finally, he further insults her by telling her to seek money from the Orangemen, meaning the Protestants. Mam attempts to restore her dignity by explaining her situation and not cowering, but Mr. Kane becomes still more cruel as the discussion continues. 5. The boys have to move in with Aunt Aggie because their mother is hospitalized. Their Aunt seems to feel it is her duty to care for the boys, even though she does it grudgingly. 6. Frank rises in the estimation of the local boys of Limerick because he has a job with Mr. Hannon delivering coal and turf; when the other boys see Frank driving the wagon, they are envious and admiring of this manly position and salary. 7. Despite claiming that he is a changed man, Dad returns at Christmas time without money or gifts and spends most of his short visit drinking. The family has the same poor Christmas meal that they have had for many years, and Dad returns to England without money or hope that he will ever conquer his alcoholism. 8. Frank comes to appreciate Shakespeare by listening to the sounds of Mrs. Purcell's radio as he sits outside on her stoop. The same radio lets Frank hear the sounds of American jazz, thus establishing a strong yearning to live in America. 9. Laman Griffin allows Mam and the children to move into his house because he realizes he can use them as servants and sexually exploit Mam.

Chapters XIII–XV

Vocabulary: 1. pithy 2. revile 3. rustics 4. succumb 5. resplendent 6. adroit 7. inviolate 8. dismal 9. vanquished

Questions: 1. Laman Griffin reneges on his promise to lend Frank the bicycle for the cycling trip to Killaloe because Frank forgets just once to empty the chamber pot; this reveals that Griffin is tyrannical and unfair since Frank usually has done his chores faithfully. 2. The teacher, Mr. O'Halloran, insists that the students memorize "The Deserted Village" because he, like the teacher in the poem, wants to inspire them with a thirst for knowledge. 3. Brother Murray of the Christian Brothers immediately rejects Frank as a candidate for placement in the school when he sees the shabby appearance of Mam and Frank. Murray is obviously a snob and is prejudiced against the poor. 4. Frank leaves Laman's house because he cannot tolerate the man's physical abuse and the sexual abuse to which his mother is victim. 5. Frank survives his stay at his Uncle Ab Sheehan's house by fending for himself and avoiding confrontation with his uncle. He avoids starving by stealing grocery deliveries from the doorsteps of wealthy people. 6. Telegrams are eagerly awaited in the poor lanes of Limerick because they usually contain money from relatives working abroad. 7. Having a steady income, although a meager one, allows Frank to bring his family to his Uncle's house and buy food for all of them. Supporting all of them will also postpone his plans to go to America.

Chapters XVI–XIX

Vocabulary: 1. e 2. f 3. b 4. g 5. a 6. c 7. d; 1. cherish 2. assiduity 3. intercede 4. perseverance 5. repose 6. languish 7. absolution

Questions: 1. Frank gets his job back because the parish priest intercedes for him by writing a letter to the postal authorities. This shows that within the Catholic community of Limerick, the priest is the ultimate authority. 2. Mrs. Finucane manages to keep up the pretense that she writes her own threatening letters to delinquent customers by hiding her association with Frank; she has him come to the back door of her building and directs him to sign the letters with her own name. 3. Uncle Pa Keating discourages Frank from taking the permanent exam that would qualify him for a job as a postman because he does not want to see his nephew fall into a mediocre and deadening life full of unsatisfactory compromises. 4. Mr. McCaffrey insists that Frank lives in a lane, rather than a street, because he wants to humiliate him; a lane is considered to be the poorest, shabbiest of residential locations. 5. The Franciscan priest helps lift a burden of guilt from Frank by granting him absolution for his relationship with Theresa Carmody and by telling Frank that Theresa's sufferings on earth assure her a place in Heaven. 6. As a magazine and newspaper distributor, Mr. McCaffrey practices censorship by tearing out sheets from periodicals that contain controversial material, such as the article on birth control that would have offended some of his Catholic customers. He does so because he considers it his duty to protect readers from corruption by "Protestant" ideas and writings. 7. Frank throws Mrs. Finucane's ledger into the river so that Limerick's poor people, including those who were friends and family, would be spared the payment of their debts on her account. This is Frank's way of making amends for writing the threatening letters for Mrs. Finucane.